Speak Now or *Forever* Hold Your Peace and *Truth*

"Say what you mean and mean it!"

Speak Now or Forever *Hold Your Peace and Truth* is all about having *"the talk."*

"For out of the overflow of the heart, the mouth speaks."
—Matthew 12:34

Speak Now or Forever Hold Your Peace and Truth
Created 2010 by Felicia Smith
© 2021

All rights reserved. No part of this book may be reproduced or transmitted in any form or by any means without written permission from the author, Felicia M. Smith, and Queen Dream Publishing.

ISBN: 978-0-9851433-4-3
Library of Congress Control:
Printed in the United States of America
"Scriptures taken from the Holy Bible®."

Disclaimer:
Although the author and publisher have made every effort to ensure the accuracy and completeness of information presented in this book, we assume no responsibility for errors, inaccuracies, omissions, or any inconsistency herein. Any slights of people, places, or organizations are unintentional.

Author's Autograph Page

To:

From:

— *Felicia Smith, MA, LPC*

Contents

Prayer	6
From the Desk of Felicia	8
Introduction	10
Chapter: Me & the Fellas (For Men)	27
Chapter: Just Us Girls (Ladies Only)	30
Chapter: Table for One "Selfie-Session"	36
Chapter: Raggedy Relationships	57
Chapter: Digital Dating	75
Dating During the Pandemic	79
Desperate Dating During the Pandemic	80

Relate-2-Connect Card Deck© Questionnaires

- Chapter: Communication — 84
- Chapter: Faith — 100
- Chapter: Family — 105
- Chapter: Finances — 112
- Chapter: Sex — 116

Meet the Author — 123

Dedication to the Many

I dedicate this book to the many who gave love a try with hopes of it maturing into a beautiful relationship or marriage, but met with failure. You are not alone. You were willing to give your heart. You were excited, drawn, overwhelmed with being sought after, pursued, and incredibly happy with your new love interest. Then things changed. Many have tried and failed and flirt with the idea of giving up, but keep going. Remember you are not alone. Do not give up, because love is worth fighting for!

"It's okay to say I do. It is important for you to know what you are saying I do to!"

Prayer for the single one-to-be-coupled

Dear God,

Thank you for past relationship lessons. Protect us from and let us not associate, affiliate, or connect with those who plan to harm, hurt, or hinder us while we interact within the relationship adjoining process. Thank you for my future blessings in the partner and spouse to come.

In Jesus name, Amen.

Guard your heart.

"Above all else, guard your heart, for everything you do flows from it."
—*Proverbs 4:23*

"Be equally yoked."
—*2 Corinthians 6:14*

Darkness is ambivalent in light.

From the Desk of Felicia

As a counselor and an advocate for healthy relationships, my academic and professional life has been dedicated to promoting in relationships sound structures that will provide a foundation for strong families. I hold a Bachelor's of Science degree in Psychology and Christian Counseling as well as an Master's degree in Marriage and Family Therapy from Liberty University. In my role as a PREPARE/ENRICH facilitator, I have advised married couples on ways to reinforce their bond, in addition to preparing couples that have yet to be married with effective strategies to ensure their union will be long, healthy, and happy. I have over thirty-five years of experience dealing with issues related to divorce and family well-being.

In addition to my work as a counselor and facilitator, I am the founder of the Relate-2-Clinic, a couples and family counseling clinic. Furthermore, I have authored numerous titles about faith, marriage, and relationships, including *Now That We've Said I Do Now What?*

Having witnessed firsthand the often-tragic results of divorce and family strife, an experience recounted in my memoir *Through the Eyes of a Daughter: Fathers We Need You*, I am deeply committed to assisting others in resolving relational and familial conflict along with achieving harmony in their marriage and family life. My personal experience, years of study, and Christian faith have strengthened my dedication to this goal. I look forward to sharing my knowledge and expertise to help you attain success in one of the most precious parts of your life, your love relationship.

God bless you as you read!

Felicia Smith, MA, LPC

Speak Now or *Forever* Hold Your Peace and *Truth*

Introduction

Single people, have a talk with your potential love interest. As my virtual mentor would say, "Dating is to gather data." This book is for the intentional audience needing to communicate real life matters that precede a committed relationship. Here you will find pointed questions that provoke in-depth conversations with your person of interest. The intent of this book is to guide you with strength and confidence to talk with you *butterfly love interest*. I describe this individual as a *butterfly love interest* because when you meet someone that strongly piques your interest, the butterfly element in your stomach may begin. Those who have experienced love before may be able to relate to this.

Alternately, it may enlighten you to the person's potential to be a great partner for you after having "*these talks.*" Do not be intimidated by the notion of "asking too many questions." Know that you are worth the investment to spend time talking *before* you decide to say, "I do." Which would you rather have: a lifetime of love or a lifetime of mystery?

Ask, seek, knock!
"Ask and it will be given to you; seek and you will find; knock and the door will be opened to you. For everyone who asks receives; he who seeks finds; and to him who knocks, the door will be opened."
—*Matthew 7:7* NIV

Ask questions; gain an understanding and make informed decisions. However, when you get answers, be able to handle the information. Ponder on this quotation below:

> *"If you can't handle my worst, you don't deserve my best!"*

Questions are the foundation of understanding. When you avoid asking, you eliminate the process of gaining vital information that you may want to know. Depending on your goal, when you do not ask, you leave things to chance. When you are intentional for marriage, you need to know a lot. Know that this type of deep communication—gaining an understanding of your potential love interest, your partner-to-be and possible spouse—is ideal and okay. The founding scripture for this book, *Matthew 12:34*, liberates you to do so. Enjoy talking to your person of interest and asking them about important things. Enjoy the process of learning about one another—seeking, if you are male, and being found, if you are female.

As you read ahead you will find questions to ask each other before you decide to date with serious intent to court, engage, and marry. You'll find suggested questions in the areas of *faith, family, sex, communication,* and *finances.* The questions offer you the opportunity to ask your person of interest, partner, or fiancé about things to know about one another during the courting process. Enjoy talking, asking, seeking—but most importantly *finding.*

> "Talking is free. Do it."
> —*Felicia Smith, MA, LPC*

> "Can two walk together unless they agree?"
> —*Amos 3:3*

"I'm looking for the one who will walk in when everyone else is walking out."

As we know, no two people are alike, and there are many differences between men and women. It is highly beneficial to find someone you can connect with in a positive manner, not only when it comes to communication but in many other aspects of the relationship. Two can walk together very well when they agree. Have you ever heard that great minds think alike? Well, they do.

> "Investigate before you invest!"
> —*My Atlanta Pastor, B.D.B.*

When you take a moment to think about investing your love, energy, effort, finances, and intentionality into a relationship, it is best to master the art of investigating, or, as we say, "gathering data." After all, dating is to gather data. This is done in a variety of ways. One of the most prominent methods of gathering information about your love interest is to effectively communicate.

While there are many methods of communicating, here we will discuss talking instead of the alternative forms of communication—such as texting, emailing, or silence, to name a few.

Being in love makes one feel wonderful, euphoric, alluring, amazing, and in bliss. I recommend taking the time to discuss relevant themes of life prior to investing your insight, attention, time, love, mind, body, soul, and heart! I will spend time educating you on a few of these matters so that you will be an informed investor in another person, but more importantly in yourself! A conversation between two agreeable parties can go a long way, either forever or only for a few moments.

Communication can go a long way in life in general. While we live in a busy society inundated with many luxuries to hurry us along on life's journey, taking the time to speak with someone of interest is vital for a healthy and lifelong relationship. Have intentional conversations with someone you view yourself pairing with in a relationship or anticipate engaging with in a lifelong commitment such as marriage. This book is not for casual acquaintances, not for sexual conquest motives, not for friends with occasional benefits or bed borrowers.

Here I define a relationship as a monogamous commitment between a woman and man. If each agrees to intend to marry one day, then this book is suited for you. While I realize other forms and structures of relationships exist in our society, I can only speak to those I believe are reflected in my personal and professional experiences.

You may be wondering how it is that I can know how important it is to have a dialogue about relevant matters when in a relationship. I have years of experience with surveying single people, have conducted a male-only survey for more than fifteen years, have experienced one failed engagement, have thirty-plus years witnessing a firsthand account of a devastating divorce and the aftereffects, have a Bachelor's of Science degree in Psychology and Christian Counseling and a Master's degree in in Marriage and Family Therapy, and have professional experience as a Counselor, working with many individuals and couples—both unmarried and married—all of which have contributed to me being able to share this knowledge with you.

Furthermore, I once owned and operated a dating firm and currently works a *Prepare * Enrich* Facilitator, helping couples to either prepare for or enrich their marriage. Most importantly, I speak from conviction and personal experience. My passion is to advocate for healthy relationships and, through the prompting of the Holy Spirit, to impart wisdom in areas which, even through pain, I have learned about relationships. I know God is love, and I am sharing what I have learned to help others to become successful in one of the most precious areas of life: love relationships.

Research, divorce statistics, wisdom, and God would say: Communication, among a few other areas I will mention, is key in a relationship. Hence, you should start with a conversation with God by praying continuously that you will make sound decisions and be opposed to inappropriate decisions that cause you pain and grief in relationships. This is so that your life will flourish in the area of love. Trust me, I know how costly foregoing prayer to make healthy and appropriate relational choices can be. Avoid that route altogether.

Therefore, let us talk and learn what we should be talking about when we come together. When you are intentional about marrying, tea, coffee, lunch, or dinner meetings with your person of interest should be intentional. If they're not, this book is for you later—when that is your relationship goal.

Understand that when you marry, you marry the person's *past, present, and future*! Having said that, communicate about the facets of life that have contributed to each stage of their life. All these parts come with them in the relationship and, ultimately, marriage. Unfortunately, you do not get to separate out or pick the parts you want to eliminate after you say, "I do." No shortcuts allowed. Therefore, why not take the time, particularly intentional time, to invest in getting to truly know the individual you have butterflies for in your belly. Yes, the butterfly effect is when you think of that person and you feel warm inside and you get that alluring feeling of excitement in your inner being or belly! You all know what I mean—well, at least those who have been in love may know.

The *butterfly effect* is a feeling that may evaporate after the euphoric phase. Typically, in the long-term phase of being in love it can last up to eighteen months. I caution some couples from marrying during this phase and before conflict so that the real fruit of the relationship has time to be birthed. More on that later. Disclaimer: all couples are different, and God is unlimited, so these are my words based on experience. I do not negate the essence of God. Pray for a lifetime of butterfly feelings that will survive the life of the relationship.

The first conversation to be had here is between you and me. We began with me asking you some thought-provoking questions. Let us call this book an interactive reading. Consider my voice to be the voice of reason, because while the butterflies are flying around in your stomach, we want you to have that feeling for a long time rather than that feeling dimming during the typical cycle of infatuation. To that end, I'll tell you a secret: the first conflict you two have will really shed light on how many of the butterflies are still there and alive.

Here are some warmup questions I have for you:

Who is the person giving you the butterflies?
Who is the *person of interest* you need to hear from day to day? That person you fall asleep talking to at night, that person you're privately texting with in your office, that person you think about on your daily commute, that person who pops into your mind at the gym. Oh, and even while you are in church during praise and worship service? Yes, who is she or he? Have you had enough conversation to gather the 3-D view of your potential love interest? Yes, the 3-D view of the person, their *past, present,* and *future*.

Have they shared with you their past, both good or bad? Things such as community, civic, or spiritual involvement, employment and educational history, political interest, jail or prison involvement (yes, you should know this)? How about former relationships: marriages, divorces, children, child support cases? What about financial information such as income tax status or assets such as existing or inherited property? And it's necessary to know their health, including STDs (I highly recommend you know this).

Yes, you should know these things—if not more—about their past, present, and future. Besides the fact that you need to know these things, those butterflies are dependent on these answers. I will go into further detail with these subjects to give you and your butterfly candidate more time to get used to actually "talking," not texting, which is not a substitution for real communication. FaceTime, Skype, Duo, or other related technology applications is not real communication either. Real face time—that is, face-to-face time spent talking—is the best form of communicating, so that facial cues are included in your conversation.

Some may caution you that you will never know everything. Yes, perhaps, but try to know enough so that your decision about *Mr. or Ms. Butterfly* is comprehensive in nature. At least ask the recommended questions in this book and you'll be sure to have a thorough view of your love interest's past, present, and future. Importantly, these questions will reveal the hard truth that make someone *reveal* or *run*. If they run and avoid, that speaks volumes. Aren't you worth the opportunity of pure unedited conversation?

Now, if you intend your connection to be casual or less than a potential marriage at some point, then this would not apply. But becoming well informed has pluses. No need for you to find out after wedding bell bliss that your *butterfly candidate* has a misdemeanor or perhaps a felony from their youth that now hinders your ability as a couple to seek out certain opportunities (e.g., living arrangements, business loans, federal financial aid for college). This could impact any of the aforementioned areas.

Or what if your butterfly love owes child support, has tax liens? What if a situation from their past is resurrected now that you two have become one (including one financial body)? I am only advocating for you to seek and enhance your knowledge, so that your decision is well informed as you grow forward together.

Let me say, too, we have all had lives before marriage. Just be well informed about that life your love interest has had prior to you. The reverse, of course, is likewise true: be honest answering these questions as well. It has been said, "What you do not know may not hurt you." As a Counselor, I would beg to differ. It never fails that a lack of knowledge or a well-informed decision sets one up for deception and, at times, a life of resentment. When it comes to knowing about life matters, it all matters, especially in a committed relationship.

Now let us talk about love for a moment. Are you aware that love is a basic human need? Let us first start with the basic human need that we all have: a yearning for Love. Yes, *the L word*. It is natural to want it, crave it, dream about it, and simply thrive on it when you are loved and loving someone of your choice and dreams. Life without love is gray, while with love it can be full of color. It is simply human nature—real human nature—not a fantasy. Besides that, God is love so it is innate for His people to follow suit with this desire.

Everyone needs love in their life. It is a *psychological* need. If you do not have, pursue it.

> "Go after a life of love as if your life depended on it, because it does."
> — *1 Corinthians 14:1*

Maslow's Hierarchy of Needs

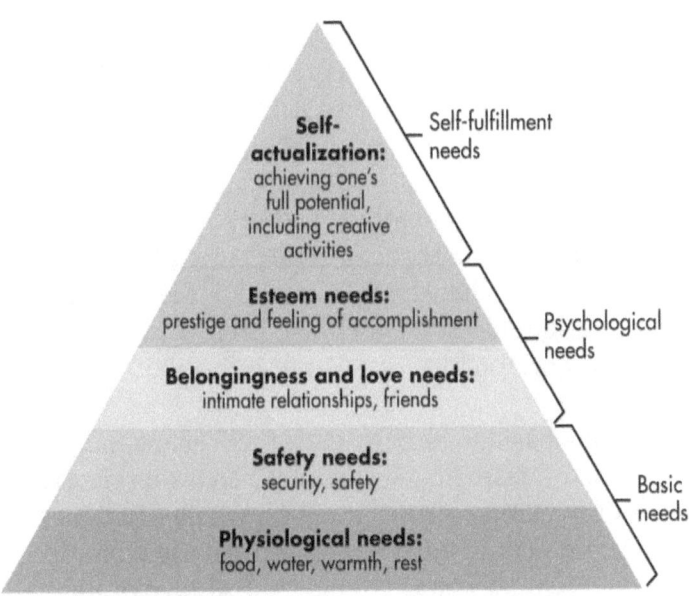

This chart of basic human needs confirms that "belongingness and love" are needs!

Love can lead to a fulfilled life. Not only is it biblical, but it is also, as we see, one of the basic human needs. *Maslow's Hierarchy of Human Needs* defines it as being "vital and important." Do not minimize the necessity of having your basic needs met.

It is a real and God-given desire to love, to be loved, and to belong. All of this is bound up with having healthy and appropriate affection. Because we so strongly desire love, we tend to stretch ourselves beyond our boundaries and become attached to someone, even if it is not in a healthy union.

The presence of love in a person's life is a vibrant and wonderful addition. Because love can be so fulfilling, life without it can be dull for some. Seek healthy love instead of the unhealthy type.

What is the goal? To seek love and see yourself having a healthy relationship that contributes to you being the best you can be. What should you avoid? Being in an unhealthy relationship that detracts from your life, health, good personality traits, and so forth.

Let us take a basic math refresher. I will share and remind you of basic math principles here as it relates to your healthy union-to-be. These basic math principles remain prominent in your life. In using basic math tips to decipher what you want to have—real love or the *illusion* of love—we can conduct the following assessment.

Add, Multiply, Divide and Subtract

Add: Assess how this individual and this relationship will add to your life. Is this person capable of satisfying your desires or needs in a relationship? If you are not entertaining a union that adds value to your life, you are likely in an unhealthy relationship. The goal should be for your union to add value to your life. This relationship should improve you or help you to be the best version of you that God designed you to be.

Subtract: What does this union take away from you? Is it a distraction from your purpose, or calling? Ask yourself: Are my productivity, quality time with God, family fun, friends, or my unique ability to authentically be me reduced by this union? No relationship should be your all, especially when it takes (subtracts) from you being the best version of you that you're destined to be.

Multiply: We are to be fruitful and to multiply (see *Genesis 9:7*). This is not opinion, it is biblical. The power of unity in a relationship is magnificent when the right two people are united. Two are better than one (see *Ecclesiastes 4:9-12*) when done right, so multiplying is inevitable.

Divide: Ask yourself, does this relationship hinder me in my salvation? Does it contribute to the good in me or the evil? We know that another person can help us to grow closer to Christ or grow further away. If a relationship divides you from your solid, founded, and core beliefs—which are Christ-focused and well-intentioned—you are likely being divided.

Really take adequate time to assess your candidate-to-be and measure them against what you really want. As I mention in my other published works, look at the applicant (butterfly candidate or person of interest) before you enter a relationship commitment just as if you are applying for a home, for a career, for a business loan, for a scholarship, or to an institution of higher education. Do some basic math and decide whether a union with him or her will add, subtract, divide, or multiply your life.

Math can be more than just numbers when applied to your relationship quality. If that person is not adding or multiplying your life, then they are subtracting and dividing who you are. They have come to compromise you, your morals, your integrity, your faith, your beliefs, and all the rest that makes you a God-centered person. *Romans 16:17-18* says, "I urge you, brothers, to watch out for those who cause division and put obstacles in your way that are contrary to the teaching you have learned. Keep away from them. For such people are not serving our Lord Christ, but their own appetites. By smooth talk and flattery, they deceive the minds of naïve people."

It is okay to date while you gather data. In a marriage-to-be relationship all data gathering for a decision should be thorough enough to make an informed decision. Get data while you date!

Reflections:

Chapter: Me & the Fellas (for Men)

"He who finds a wife finds a good thing and obtains favor from the Lord."
—*Proverbs 18:22*

Men, be real with ladies. If you are not interested, be honest and let her know. Have a conscience and be honest with someone when they are showing interest in return. As we hear, there are a surplus of women seeking their hand to be sought in marriage. That said, if you know that is not what you are looking for then be honest with her. This section is short in the book because women are seeking resources to better save on their time, energy, and efforts of being found by The One. Keep it real and keep it moving if you are not kingdom-minded, in that you are seeking a real relationship of substance and not seeking vagina only! Help her save her heart. Be a hero in this regard! This is for men looking for a wife, not for those looking for hedonism in the world these days.

We get it, some are only about *that life*, as we say, but a man looking for a wife can find that in today's world. They are plenty of vivacious, smart, intelligent, kind, witty, saved, and honest women that exist. When you find her do not exchange quantity for quality in the dating game. Please, I beseech you to take her seriously at first glance so you will not forsake your future for present "games" being offered or available to you.

Reflections:

Chapter: Just Us Girls (Ladies Only)

> "Above all else, guard your heart,
> for everything you do flows from it."
> —*Proverbs 4:23*

Now ladies, it is just us talking. When you are gathering information through conversation, be mindful to guard your heart. Pray and ask God if you are a believer before each encounter to protect your heart. Talking can become intimate, or, if you're not careful, a soul-tie. An emotional soul-tie can easily form from sharing some of these heart matters. Be mindful to guard your heart until the peace of God allows you to settle matters with this person who could potentially become your spouse. Ladies you are powerful! Girls really do run the world. We have babies, remember.

But seriously, let's say a man shows interest. Mr.-Right-for-Someone-Else will show you subpar interest, ladies. When you are seen by the *right* man, he will not only tell you he is interested in you, but he will demonstrate his interest to match. My Atlanta Bishop, Bishop D. Bronner, mentioned years ago in a sermon that "you don't have to pursue who's already attracted to you." So, ladies, if you are seeing something different, ask yourself: Do you want to invest in, wait for, pursue, or chase someone who is treating you less than desirably? Invest only where the feeling is mutual.

It could be the timing of things that has his interest somewhere else. Nevertheless, if is not the right time, move ahead with your life, goals, and purpose. A man, when he sees you, will come for you. You are not missing anything that belongs to you that will not remain in your life on its own! It is better to let go and really let God, trust me!

Women are being referred to now as "thirsty" in terms of getting involved with men. From research, it seems like more than the word "thirsty." It is more like dehydrated when it comes to today's dating dynamics. Spend some time investing in yourself so that you will present yourself as the jewel you are. Present something elegant and classy—your queen-worthiness. That means getting answers up front (*real queens ask questions*).

More on that. Ladies, when you get to the point of deciding that you no longer want to be involved with him, be okay with moving on. It is okay for you to observe, ask questions, and move on when the situation is not right for you. Moving on means not looking back. Start by communicating that this it is not what you want, and then close the door. Closing the door means no longer resuscitating the dead, no longer breathing life into a situation that is lifeless.

It has been said that "there are plenty of fish in the sea." There are killer whales and sharks in the sea, too. Prior to casting your net again, be sure to know your worth. Be okay with moving on from a place that does not work for you!

5 strategies for moving on:

- Decide to move on (refocus)
- Believe you are worth what you want (restructure)
- Improve your self-image (rebrand)
- Improve your net worth (rebuild)
- Improve your spiritual life (recover)

Ecclesiastes 3:3-8

³ a time to kill and a time to **heal**,
a time to tear down and a time to **build,**
⁴ a time to weep and a time to laugh,
a time to mourn and a time to dance,
⁵ a time to scatter stones and a time to gather them,
a time to embrace and a time to ***refrain from embracing,***
⁶ a time to search and a ***time to give up***,
a time to keep and a ***time to throw away***,
⁷ a time to tear and a ***time to mend***,
a time to be silent and a time to speak,
⁸ a time to love and a time to hate,
a time for war and a time for peace.

Reflect on the scriptures and strategies above. Let us begin by deciding to refocus your attention on getting healing. It is okay to take a break to reflect, refresh, and refocus. Rebuild your net worth. That means refocusing yourself and refraining from the negative aspects of a relationship in order to improve your net worth, employment situation, or business ownership status. Consider rebuilding your self-image by exercising or seeking counseling if you struggle with mental health challenges or traumas that are impacting your ability to complete necessary tasks.

Restructure by trusting God to help you with the timing of giving up, throwing away, and mending. Healing and recovery from a breakup or an upgrade in relationship lifestyle requires change. Change is a process and a pursuit! Your mindset and daily habits determine the change you are pursuing—whether it is your past, present, or future. Pursue your future with effective changes. Ladies, God can give you the desires of your heart. To get better results, trust God to seek salvation and put your best efforts into believing in yourself. Use these strategies to refocus, rebuild, restructure, rebrand, and recover from the grip of any less than desirable relationship.

"For no good thing does he withhold from those whose walk is blameless."
—*Psalms 84:11* NIV

"Go forward, get better!"

Reflections:

Chapter: Table for One "Selfie-Session"

"When you're peaceful, you're powerful."
—*Joyce Meyers*

Walk in peace with the knowledge you gain from these "talks." It is wonderful to have the peace in your heart that you know what you need to know about from good, open communication. Instead of using the first couple of dates to go to a movie, why not challenge yourself to meet at a coffee shop of your choice and converse with this book as an aid or use the *Relate-2-"Connect" Card Deck©*. Talk with one another. Yes—sit and talk the first few times you get together. More importantly, ask a few questions and get a few answers so that you began conversing and communicating up front.

Know that divorce statistics indicate that more than 55% of divorces are from first time marriages. That is real! A lack of communication has an alarming impact on this statistic, according to research. Talking should precede meeting, greeting, dating, or marrying an individual. Some think asking questions up front may be intimidating, but I encourage you to take responsibility for *knowing* instead of assuming that you and your love interest have similar thoughts, hobbies, and—most importantly—faith-based preferences.

This part of the book is a discussion between you and me. Yes, let's talk about some things before you take the opportunity to discuss matters of the heart with someone you may want to consider growing forward with. Have you taken inventory of where you are in terms of the ideal relationship that fits your lifestyle? Where are you in your life when it comes to faith, finances, communication, family, and sex? Research indicates these are leading divorce causes, so we will focus on these specific areas in this data gathering experience.

Where are you in your faith walk? How important is this area of your life? Have you considered how important this area should be in a dating relationship with the potential to marry? Be honest with yourself in this area as well as in those to follow.

What about your finances? It has been said that those without assets hoping to gain access to another's assets in dating relationships means that they are "gold digging." Survey your own assets and finances to see what they look like.

What is your communication style? How do you prefer to be reached in terms of communication? Take time to know so that, when the right relationship presents itself, you can be honest (and not cause injury) to your *person of interest* or *butterfly* candidate. For example, do you prefer talking or texting? Are you a visual communicator? Do you need to FaceTime or meet face-to-face in person?

What about family? Are you in contact with your family? What are your ideas for having a family? Are you single with children wanting to date? Do you want to marry someone without children?

Even if you are with a childless partner, this still does not eliminate the aspect of dealing with family issues as it relates to the in-laws. For those who of you open to dating and marrying one with children, consider your family background as well as that of your person of interest (POI). The *Instafam* (the instant family when you marry) will be a blended family, so this requires special attention. We will go further into this special family dynamic in the family section of this book.

Below are your solo questions for you. Think of it as a "selfie-session where we will address *you* before we get into the couple questionnaires. For now, ponder the following sections and reflect inwardly on your responses. At times, your responses may be an indicator of whether you are ready to move forward in a serious relationship with the potential or intent to marry or if you still need time to heal. You're welcome to take notes in between questions to really reflect on what comes up for you.

Use this book and accompanying *Relate-2-"Connect" Card Deck©,* as a guide to help you ask the questions you may otherwise be too timid to ask. Let this book and card deck serve as a guide to wisdom and to help formulate the discussions you should be having with a future partner. Essentially your responses to questions should help to encourage whether you should proceed or not. The responses your love interest provides during these discussions may help each of you to determine whether or not this is the right partner for your future.

It is best to first be happy before entering a relationship and then take happy with you into the relationship. It is especially important to be healed from past relationships and not to hold on to past brokenness. Being broken will show up with you and be just as visible as your physical self.

People are not irreplaceable, and God is the only true healer. A relationship, while it may make you happy, still is not a cure for previous baggage. Bondage and any issues you previously encountered are still there until you proactively seek healing before presenting yourself to a strong potential mate.

When you get to the questionnaire about purpose and employment, be mindful. You may need to show compassion if your love interest possesses less clarity of purpose. People can be "threatened by your purpose when they do not know their own purpose." Adam knew his purpose, so it was easy for Eve to be his helper. When your partner does not know their God-given purpose, your drive, focus, and intentionality may be a challenge for them to understand. In such circumstances, you have innate gifts, so be mindful and take this into consideration.

This can also apply to your partner's spiritual life. While they may not know their own purpose for life, it is vital to your personal success to know yours. Since this book is intended for emotionally mature readers, the goal for any relationship is marriage. Consider these ideas in relation to marriage making your life better. In marriage you should develop into the best person God has called you to be. Achieving that depends on your spouse, too.

An effective marriage demands spouses who complement one another. I would venture to say that, while we may live on earth, some marriages are truly made in heaven. There are challenges in every marriage, but the couple that truly complement one another have a marriage that is heaven sent.

As we say in the Christian community, if God is not going to get the blessing or glory from your union, you have to ask yourself: Is this heaven sent or is it perhaps hell sent? Determine if this relationship complements who you are and who your partner is. Or is the relationship a compromise of your principles or based on a private competition with someone else or another couple?

The above and below questions will help you see which kind of relationship you have or will have. You should spend time getting to know your *love interest* as soon as possible by knowing as much as necessary to make a conscious decision. There is nothing wrong with being assertive as it relates to a *person of interest*, provided they agree with where the relationship might be headed. This could be the best decision you make in your life. Invest your time, efforts, and energy wisely—but ask questions!

As you prepare to learn information about your *person of interest*, be mindful of protecting what you learn. Protect your relationship in this embryonic stage, too. In other words, do not tell all your business to your friends and family during this phase. If this has been your norm in the past, reflect on doing things differently this time. Protect the information because those you tell may not be as forgiving as you are of what you learn during these conversations. This is just a word of suggestion for you.

"Be in a hurry to go nowhere fast!"

Learn and leave, quicker than sticking and staying! But again, learn and leave if you need to!

Reflections:

Faith

1. What do I believe about God?

2. What faith community do I affiliate with?

3. What do I prefer my partner's religious or faith preference to be? Similar or the same?

4. Am I okay with dating or marrying a partner of opposite faith preferences?

5. If I marry someone of a different faith or belief perspective, how might this impact our relationship?

Notes: _____

_____

Finances

1. Where am I financially?

2. What is my concept of money?

3. Do I have enough money to live independently regardless of my relationship status?

4. Am I comfortable marrying someone with less financial status than me?

5. Am I okay with dating or marrying a partner that believes each partner should split bills in the household 50/50?

Notes: _____

_____

Family

1. Am I healed from, if any, childhood trauma?

2. Do I have mother issues that I am still hurting from?

3. Do I have any daddy issues that I am still hurting from?

4. Are there any family secrets that might affect my relationship?

5. What are my views of family?

Notes: _____

_____

Communication

1. What is my personality type?

2. What is my love language?

3. What is my preferred method of communication?

4. Am I an effective communicator?

5. What about the way I communicate has caused me problems in past relationships?

Notes: _____

_____

Sex

1. What is my sexual ideology?

2. What are my views on sex before marriage?

3. What are my thoughts about sex within marriage?

4. Am I open minded when it comes to sex? If so, how? If not, what are some reasons why?

5. Am I open to communicating honestly about sex with my partner?

Notes: _____

_____

Bonus *Selfie-Session* questions:

1. Do I love myself?

2. What do I love about myself?

3. What do I dislike about myself?

4. What unfinished relationship issues do I have?

5. Am I holding a grudge against anyone that I was once in a relationship with?

6. What, if any, unaddressed mental health matters am I in need of support for?

7. Have I had any sexual interest outside of monogamy in the past that hinders me?

8. What health issues do I have that could impact my relationship? (This includes sexual health in the fullest sense.)

9. Do I have any terminally ill family health issues that might need to be addressed?

10. What do I want to improve about myself?

11. What do I want to accomplish before I get into a committed relationship?

12. Am I ready to merge my life with another person's?

13. Why do I want to be in a relationship?

14. What baggage do I bring to the relationship?

15. What do I want to be different in my relationship that I experienced in my family life?

16. What is my personal vision for my life?

17. Am I satisfied in my career?

18. Do I really like my job?

19. What educational goals do I still want to complete?

20. Is having a relationship too much of a sacrifice in my life as I currently live it?

21. Will a relationship be a complement to my life?

22. What vision do I have for my future mate? (*Habakkuk 2:2*)

23. Do I want children?

Notes: _____

_____

_____

I pray this section has given you an opportunity to reflect on where you are in these areas prior to your union with *Mr. or Ms. Butterfly*, your *person of interest*. We all come into relationships with past concerns and issues, so you don't need to concern yourself with not being accepted. As we mature, we come into relationships with a past life. Some call this baggage. It's common for individuals to have something in their past that presents itself as an issue, including a family history that is less than perfect.

Examples of such baggage includes children, debt, criminal records, health issues, divorce, tax issues, child support issues, religious bondage, and addictions. The longer you live, the more understanding you and your *love interest* need to be and the more necessary it is that you have compassion towards yourself when answering the solo questionnaires. You can choose whether or not to accept the responses of your partner-to-be, but it is best to be thoroughly informed. The questionnaires are specifically designed to accomplish this—they are thorough questions that will provoke in-depth conversations within yourself and with your person of interest.

For some, past errors, struggles, and bondage can be referred to as baggage. Some are lighter than others, but the more you talk to yourself and reflect, the more you can easily talk with another about baggage—both yours and theirs. Now let me note this disclaimer, if you are too young to date (prior to young adulthood) or consider marriage, this conversation is not applicable to you at this stage. The conversation I'm suggesting is very much for those who have lived their lives and acquired things along the path of life. This conversation is designed for mature individuals who have experiences in life and are looking for a long-term partnership such as marriage.

> "For out of the overflow of the heart, the mouth speaks."
> *Matthew 12:34*

You have the power to negotiate what you want to entertain in your marriage before you say, "I do."

I repeat: take the time to ask questions.

When you do discover things, you may not be able to live with, pray about your next steps. If you find that your love interest has a past that seems to be unacceptable, per your standards, find out if these are deal breakers or things in which you are willing to compromise. Realize that these issues are not *your* issues, just things that have surfaced of which your love interest has informed you.

Meeting someone of interest is one thing, but true possibilities for the future are measure by meeting someone you measure in terms of their potential as a true relationship partner. Perhaps that relationship will ultimately lead to marriage. Unless you have such a love interest in mind, this book would be used on the wrong person, and at an inopportune time—although your reading could help with shedding light on those who you should not further consider as love interests.

This is an effective method for aligning the peace in your heart with new information about your butterfly interest. There are things you will need to know about your love interest and peace will be a guide.

But peace is ineffective when your decision making is faulty. Instead of taking a few rounds of dates to go to a movie, why not challenge yourself to a meet and greet at a coffee house and talk with one another. Bring this book or card deck for a guide to steer that conversation. Yes, sit and talk the first few times you get together. More importantly, get answers to a few basic questions asked so that you can begin learning about your love interest up front.

Divorce statistics are reported as 55% for first time marriages. The divorce rates go higher for second and third marriages, so communication must take precedence when we meet. Gather data while you date, and *before* you marry.

Some think asking questions up front may be intimidating. Take responsibility for inquiring about your partner's interests and past history instead of assuming that you and this perfectly unknown person have similar thoughts, interests, hobbies, and faith-based preferences.

Do not buy into the famous slogan "time will tell all." Why not ask *now*? The Bible justifies asking questions. "You have not because you ask not," according to *James 4:2*.

If you do elect to come together, consider bringing in a trusted fellow couple you can talk to when things go awry in your relationship. This couple can serve the role of a marriage mentor.

Reflections:

Table for two

Eat, but talk too! Ask questions and gain an understanding of your person of interest.

"My people are destroyed from lack of knowledge."
—*Hosea 4:6*

Chapter: Raggedy Relationships

"It is what it is but it's not what it shall be."
—*Rubye Jones Hall*

Question: What are you looking for in a relationship? The way of the world has changed immensely, and so has the way of dating—which is called "courting" for those who hold on to the Christian way of dating and its nostalgic verbiage, though the two are sequential in nature. The term "courting" is used in the Christian faith community, while "dating" is an obviously secular term and lifestyle. When you are in the "of this world" mindset and do not regard Christian principles in your love life, you understand that "dating" is synonymous with an opaque lifestyle.

This chapter is dedicated to some of the common terms and situations individuals encounter in the secular dating arena.

These types of default arrangements occur when a couple has not solidified their relationship. For instance, have you heard someone mention they are in a *"situationship"*? What about the phrase *"It's complicated"*? When is it ever okay for a relationship that involves your time, your heart, and your soul to be complicated? I ask because this is what some entertain when it comes to relationship status. Of course, the goal is to have a substantial relationship that is honorable—at least that is the audience this book is intended for and those are the individuals I'm sharing with here. If you are of the mindset that any of the following six raggedy relationship styles are acceptable, then use this book to better inform yourself. The individuals I intend to speak to are those that are serious about leaving the current world's dating standards behind in exchange for finding a suitable partner to honor the God-given intention of marriage.

Situationship or *It's complicated* is the first raggedy relationship in which both have components of a relationship but without giving the respect and honor of being identified as such. One of the reasons individuals compromise and involve themselves in these types of relationships is that one of the two is not fully available, whether that means they're still married, just divorced, recently separated, or simply weighing their options. Why else would they want you to be a sideline priority while they figure out what they want? Take a survey of who you are. Are you accepting such a relationship because you feel subpar? (By the way, stringing yourself along for years while you call yourself someone's "friend" as they use you as though they're your significant other falls in this category as well.)

They use you while they are still married, or currently separated and not legally divorced, or living in two households while still married. Perhaps they live with the father or mother of their child. If so, they are dating for the sake of convenience. Banish from your mind the notion that you can form a solid relationship with them. You see, they are already in a relationship that has not ended, especially if still married. Though they are physically and practically with you often—possibly every day—legally they are not available to pursue you in marriage. Facts!

What I'm asking you to embrace is a very stringent relationship between you and God. Please understand that God can provide you with a "free and clear" partner that is 100% available to pursue or be pursued. Press "delete" on the many raggedy relationship arrangements that exist in the present day. It used to be simple. Boy meets girl, girl answers the love note: "Do you like me, yes or no?" Nowadays, however, the world has blemished what should essentially be pure. That is the work of Satanism.

The second raggedy relationship style that exists is *"friends with benefits."* What you have here is all the ingredients of a relationship, but you are only calling one another friend. Again, ask yourself the same question: What makes you exchange your time, effort, availability, interests, feelings, and sometimes soul without upgrading this arrangement to a relationship of honor?

It's understandable to meet someone and pursue a healthy part of a friendship with the intent of becoming a couple for a brief period. But when you get into years of this style of relationship, with only some of the traits of being a couple, you need to reflect on what makes you remain instead of taking a leap of faith into a relationship.

The third raggedy relationship style is "*side chick, side piece, boy toy, maintenance man*," etc. These are exactly what they are—a mistress or lover that knowingly is a third wheel to a married couple! This role is one which comes with stigma attached. No matter the exterior, no matter the tangible benefits involved in this arrangement (especially with a married person), there is unavoidable damage when you attach yourself in such a demonic manner. You see, on the outside the arrangement seems pretty, and wrapped with a bow around it, but there are consequences and risk involved when you intrude on an unresolved marriage.

The fourth raggedy relationship style is that of the *"entanglement."* This consists of three or more people aware of their role in the relationship arrangement. An entanglement is defined as a situation or relationship that you are involved in that is hard to escape.

According to statistics, this one may be of the most destructive relationship arrangements, the reason being that crime statistics suggest that this arrangement really does not work. Do your research on "entanglements homicides" and you'll see that when you cross the boundaries in this style of relationship as a knowing third wheel, you settle for crossing a spiritual boundary. Marriage is holy. It is sacred between man and woman. When shared, the marriage bed becomes defiled, spiritually if not physically. Read *Hebrews 13:4* in your Bible for more information in this area but, briefly, you will see consequences when you involve yourself in an "entanglement." It seems okay if everyone in the "entanglement" knows but someone, if not everyone, will pay the price. Sometimes that price is death, other times it is longing, after your exit, for the person you couldn't have all for yourself.

"It's either all or nothing."

Do not settle for just something. Unless you want to entertain a raggedy relationship.

Number five of the six raggedy relationship styles is the relationship with a *"narcissist."* A narcissist is defined as an individual that is diagnosed with a personality disorder. This personality type, by clinical definition, is one that:

1) Has a grandiose sense of self-importance
2) Is preoccupied with fantasies of unlimited power, success, brilliance, beauty, or ideal love
3) Believes he or she is special and unique
4) Requires excessive admiration
5) Has a sense of entitlement
6) Is personally exploitative
7) Lacks empathy
8) Is often envious of others
9) Shows arrogant, haughty behaviors of attitude

For one to be diagnosed with narcissism one must have met the current American Psychiatric Association DSM-5 criteria. This is usually done through a clinical evaluation by a licensed professional such as a Counselor, Clinical Social Worker, Marriage & Family Counselor, Psychologist, or Psychiatrist. Again, these professionals are trained, educated, and licensed individuals in the clinical arena. To identify a narcissist based on their behaviors above is an impression the "coaches" are making of an individual based on collected individual experiences.

Now that you see this clinical definition, how does it measure up against what you may have perceived about being involved with a narcissist? What do you think? Many are spending time on social media coaching on narcissism because it is more common to have been involved in this type of relationship as of late. I will offer you a short glossary of some of the non-clinical terms associated with a narcissistic relationship. Please know that these are non-clinical terms and behaviors that have been coined by online coaches concerning dating a narcissist. These are identifiable behaviors that have been linked to narcissism.

1) *Narcissist supply*
    o   Men or women dating a narcissist.
2) *Love bombing*
    o   Bestowing gifts on you at the onset of the relationship.
3) *Gaslighting*
    o   Reverse psychology that manipulates you into believing *you* are the "crazy" one.
4) *Mirroring*
    o   Replicating what they see or think you like them doing. They do this to entice you to date them or stay with them.
5) *Monkey branching*
    o   Moving from a relationship with you to one with someone else (their new "supply") and back to you if possible.

6) *Discarded*
    - Dumping you.

If you have been in a relationship with a narcissist then God bless you. Hopefully, the brief glossary of behaviors associated with a narcissist relationship is helpful and revelatory in nature. If you have been victimized by unhealthy dynamics involving a narcissist you may benefit from professional counseling.

A narcissist in a relationship—sometimes referred to as a "transaction"—can mimic inhumane behaviors. At times you may notice the narcissist bullying you. They initiate discussion by pointing out your errors or shortcomings. Sadly, these discussions display zero sense of the narcissist taking ownership of their own issues due to their sense of entitlement. Know that this heightens your inability to say "no" to demands, which for this personality disorder is a "no-no." Often, they may present the impression that *they* are the victim in the relationship due to *your* wrongs. They bully, love to argue, and love to be a victim! When you engage in conflict or lean into this behavior you supply fuel for their sense of self and their insecurity. Narcissists need constant validation. You are a prime "supplier" when you reinforce this superficial and fragile confidence.

You may be unaware of their narcissism at the beginning of the relationship because the love bombing and mirroring resembles a beautiful relationship-to-be, but if you are in a unilateral relationship that only works when you are reinforcing toxic behavior, superficial validation, or air-filled, cloudy, attention-seeking behavior, you are the "supply" in a transactional narcissistic relationship.

Survey who you are and take stock of your self-value. When you are driven by prevailing relationship standards, any of the aforementioned "raggedy relationships" are less than desirable if you seek a healthy marriage to come. Aside from the damage it can cause to you, you also increase the damage to others by playing a role in any of these relationships. You must realize that you reap what you sow (otherwise known as karma). Keep that in mind when you are ready to seek a relationship of honor. For some, dating one-on-one is a retro notion and, again, if this is the case, this is not the book for you—especially if you subscribe to any of the previous notions of a *raggedy relationship*. I encourage you to reconsider your appetite for any of that!

When your intimacy appetite accommodates such lifestyles, you essentially plant a seed into your future that may be more costly than you realize. Intertwining with others from a sexual standpoint creates a soul tie. A soul tie is defined as "a spiritual connection between two people. In many cases, it is said to come into existence after two people have been physically intimate. In others, it is said to form after an intensely close spiritual or emotional relationship." It is no wonder that when the relationship is over there is a longing for that individual. It is not surprising that the tearing of these relationships is injurious in nature.

When you connect in the spirit with another believer, on the other hand, you inherit the blessings that comes from having a respectful, structured relationship. You inherit the blessings of the covenant in marriage. God, Jesus, and the Holy Spirit are joining you in marriage as a couple. But when you exploit yourself as a booty call, or as a "friend with benefits," Satan becomes your relative or father-in-law-to-be if you ultimately marry into such a relationship!

Count the cost of your involvement. Consider *Matthew 7:6*, which states, "Do not give what is holy to the dogs; nor cast your pearls before swine, lest they trample them under their feet, and turn and tear you in pieces." If you are a believer, you must understand the power of influence and the consequence of interacting with those who are of opposing beliefs. If you really want a partner that shares similar beliefs, be certain and clear about the influence of these beliefs and go for what you believe in. To do otherwise—to give into something not of your preference—can place you in a dangerous position if you're not careful.

Talk with your partner-to-be about your differences but understand that those who are led by the devil will want you to comply with their request to give in to their fleshly desires, even when they come to you incredibly attractive and with an insurmountable amount of swag. Demons are well packaged, but the truth remains: this is Satanic if you look carefully. I want to encourage you to not give in to tricks packaged in "fine" or "swag" for your salvation, my friend. Consider and weigh, don't gamble. The power of sexual influence, convenience, and settling is real! This is especially important for those who have been waiting for quite some time for the right person and have yet to have that special person show up. When you have no one, it is easy to be on guard when someone comes into your life. Be sufficiently spiritually grounded. This will help Satan's lies to not temp you beyond your moral and spiritual compass. Wait for it to show up. It is worth your time. Do not lose focus of what is at stake when considering whether or not to "give in" to these temporary fragments of relationships that cost so much. Stay focused on the purpose God has for you and don't be tempted to lose focus on Kingdom living and the unedited truth in the Word of God, the Bible.

The story of Rachel and Jacob is profound. *Genesis 29:20* clearly describes how Jacob and Leah both paid a cost to be in a fruitful relationship. Jacob more than Leah paid the cost because he worked to ensure that he would get his bride after a period of long toil.
The cost is this: wait until you say "I do" for the covenant blessings of marriage. Too many people want to skip making the covenant and live as husband and

wife (playing house) instead of including God in the relationship. Do not give the benefits of marriage to another before they have paid the cost to have you. Surely there are many types of relationships available to have you and your pearls for free. The question and decision becomes whether you will allow them to.

Jacob worked fourteen years to have the woman he desired as his wife. That may seem an exceptionally long time, but it actually isn't that long when you think of being happy with your mate—the right one at that—for the rest of your lives together.

If you are struggling in a relationship which you know is not of God and is filled with sin, lust, and premarital sex, please read the following verses at the end of this chapter to inform you of some principle's worth considering. Each person's history is different, so we want to provide you with some encouragement to know that God has a plan for you. He has in mind your salvation, your purpose in life, and the covenant of marriage, which begins with dating. You are worth more than going to hell over relationships.

If this has been your struggle, repent and ask God for His forgiveness, grace, and mercy but realize that you may suffer the consequences of living a sin-filled life. No one is worth losing your salvation over. You must understand that if you believe in God and have confessed Jesus as your savior then you belong to God.

I would encourage you to consider the idea of no longer trading belief for a first-class ticket to hell because you want to temporarily gratify the flesh in hopes of gaining a spouse. If your traditional method of dating includes being intertwined with individuals expecting elements of an impure relationship, consider your salvation when determining your actions. I realize this is a challenge and societal pressures suggest otherwise. The Bible is clear on how this is handled. The world's standards are not superior to God! Consider in the following scriptures what God says to you in your quiet time:

"For no good thing does he withhold from those whose walk is blameless."
—*Psalms 84:11*

"But those who hope in the Lord will renew their strength. They will soar on wings like Eagles; they will run and not grow weary; they will walk and not be faint."
—*Isaiah 40:31*

Moving on to our last raggedy relationship, number six, is the one known as *"Mr. or Ms. Housecalls."* This individual goes from house to house exploiting themselves and their self-respect in ways that, at times, end up creating children. Yes, they go from house to house using bodies in exchange for sexual feelings and lust. It really is self-exploitation, because you voluntarily exploit yourself and lower your self-worth by going from house to house, using others or allowing yourself to be used. In the meantime, semen and bodily fluids are left as evidence, which at times results in children or unplanned pregnancies. Such individuals are only seeking to soothe temporary needs without regard for the life that may come from these actions. There is no emotional, financial, spiritual, psychological, or familial investment in you on any level. An arrangement with *Mr. or Ms. Housecalls* is only physical in nature! If that is all you seek, read the scriptures, and reflect on what God would say about this.

This is the type of relationship that is only available for a *housecall* (aka booty call) as long as you are still available to be used. Once their needs are fulfilled, they are gone. For those of you too vulnerable for something of this magnitude, do not subject yourself to this arrangement, which has traits similar to that of the *situationship* and *friends with benefits*. All of these take on the notion that "we live together, or are friends that use each other for sex, but we have no commitment. We are free to do whatever we want with whomever we want." However, one deception of these raggedy relationships is the fact that emotions can appear in the form of jealousy. When this happens, often you will see the situation change because—guess what has been developing the entire time: the relationship! Stop playing games with your life, your body, and your status. Status, you say? Yeah, your HIV status. And nowadays, your COVID-19 status.

If you struggle with entertaining raggedy relationships, please know you are worthy of going beyond being someone's "option." It's healthy to *decide* not to be an "option" for anyone and to make yourself a priority, but to truly achieve it takes work. If you demonstrate that you are a priority, people will adjust to how you treat yourself and either respect that or run. If they run, thank yourself for a missed headache in advance. When meeting individuals, it is vital that you use discernment when deciding if you are to move forward with them. In the world this is known as "women's intuition" or as "my gut told me so."

Discernment and intuition are synonymous with prayer because God will show you when you seek Him and carefully and diligently reflect on what to do. If, that is, you are a believer. Out in the world or in other religions these standards are different. More often than not, if you are referring to your relationship status as complicated or asking yourself or others what you should do, then you are not 100% the priority in the relationship. "Fear and faith" are not roommates. The relationship that comes to complete or complement you will not compete with your morals, your standards, or your integrity. It is not a bad idea to consult God to find out if this relationship or situation presented to you is a detour, also known as a distraction. Whenever you are purposeful, focused on your career, or otherwise occupied with positive things, distractions in the form of relationships also show up. Be aware and be mindful. Stay focused on what you are believing for!

> "Be secure with telling that person that you are believing for a Christian marriage."

> "If you follow Christ, I will follow you."
> —*Pastor Tony Evans*

If you need to recover from limiting yourself in raggedy relationships, consider the following: seek healing and wholeness to recover and be restored from these raggedy relationships.

The first step in getting healed, aside from prayer and asking God for help, is to "decide to let go and do not look back." Dating terminology refers to this as ghosting. Please learn more about ghosting as you read the Digital Dating chapter ahead. In my book *Seeds of Hope*, I mention that an exit does not need an introduction when you are entertaining a *booty call*, *situationship*, *"it is complicated,"* entanglement, *side piece, side chick, boy toy, male lover,* or *friend with benefits* arrangement. These relationship types are raggedy.

"Follow the ways of your heart and whatever your eyes see but know that for all these things God will bring you to judgement."
—*Ecclesiastes 11:9*

"Do what you have to do until you can do what you want to do."
—*Denzel Washington*

"Quitting ahead is not the same as quitting."

"One must take the time to assess their situation."

Loving You is letting Go
Please reflect on the following scripture and quote as you consider moving forward.

"Do not give dogs what is sacred; do not throw your pearls to pigs. If you do, they may trample them under their feet, and turn and tear you to pieces."
—*Matthew 7:6*

Reflections:

Chapter: Digital Dating

"Clicking for companionship."

"Don't chase a computer mouse (online dating) in search of getting your spouse."

God knows exactly where you are. He knows your address, He knows what car you drive, He knows where you work and serve. After all, God is sovereign, remember, and He knows all and can do all. Trust Him to put you on the right path to receive you partner. WAIT for it.

How does the above opening statement sound? Antiquated, I know, but it's actually more salient than ever. This book is being published during an era of pandemic due to the coronavirus (COVID-19). Online dating is the premier way of connecting with individuals, especially if you are currently required to quarantine and socially distance.

Asking questions is now more important than ever, but just because you ask questions and hear the "right" answer does not mean that the response is *true*. You know how it is when you go in for an interview: whether you have been the interviewer or interviewee, responses to questions can be formulated in a way that *seems* correct. You will not know for some time to come if the responses are accurate. Time will show what the reality of the response truly is. Ask, observe, and see what is demonstrated.

Here are some immediate tips for digital dating:

> - Ask the *right* questions up front, the questions you want answered (e.g., relationship status)
> - Advocate for yourself
>   - Exercise safety, use boundaries as needed (e.g., personal safety)
> - Do not waste time texting on an app when you can talk
>   - If you do not want to continue texting, say so (advocate for yourself!)
> - Recognize ghosting when it occurs
>   - Ghosting is an abrupt communication halt. The other person has walked away without notice.
> - Make no contact after a breakup
>   - Make no contact with the individual who is no longer in contact with you (this is hard but has long-term benefits)

When you are leading the conversation, discern if the conversation is one-sided. Are they reciprocating by asking you questions as well? If they are not reciprocating, consider whether or not they are equally interested in you. A unilateral conversation raises questions about validity of "a relationship in progress." Could this actually be a potential *raggedy relationship*? Remember that an interested person shows interest and often that is done through conversation. Inquiring, asking questions, and showing as much if not more interest in you. When you are the one often starting the stream of conversation, you might be the more interested person. Leaving aside some obvious considerations—is the person introverted or shy? — interest should be balanced, and a given on both sides. If you never said anything, would they say something? Be mindful—especially you ladies who are on social media platforms—when you are *clicking for companionship*.

Reflections:

Digital Dating During a Pandemic

"Being in a relationship is taking a chance, risk & work."
—*Ceola Evans*

Online dating can be beneficial for the individual balancing their career, life, family, etc. Digital dating can be convenient for the savvy user, especially during the current pandemic. Moving from digital dating to in-person meetups should include:

- Wearing a mask
- Practicing social distancing
- Using hand sanitizer often
- Considering wearing gloves
- Limiting physical contact
- Meeting safely in a mutual location (e.g., park, outside bistro, coffee house)
- Texting or sharing your location with a friend

Desperate Dating During the Pandemic

Ladies and gentlemen, you are worth waiting for and worth fighting for! Present yourself as such. Remember, there is an adage that says, "there are a lot of fish in the sea," but sharks are in the sea too! Be mindful to stay prayed up as you date and discover who may be your person of interest. Why? Because while some pray, others prey! As *Proverbs 4:23* says, "guard your heart" while they earn the privilege of capturing it. Desperate dating during the pandemic demonstrates recklessness with your heart, but also with your health. Spend time talking and getting an understanding of who this newfound person of interest is during this time. We want to lessen your thirsty activities, your dehydrated dating tactics, which can mimic desperation when you do not take the necessary time to effectively date for value.

Reflections:

As previously mentioned, "the one asking questions is the one pursuing the relationship." Inquiring about a new love interest and asking questions, along with showing interest, is bilateral when done right.

"It takes two to tangle."

Reflections:

Relate-2-Connect Card Deck©
"Communication"

"Queens ask questions. Kings have answers."
—*Pastor R.C. Blakes*

Communication is essential in relationships. It is one of the congruence principles to a successful relationship. If communication is a challenge for you, learn to do so ahead of time. Being an effective communicator saves you time, especially when conflict arises. Not *if* conflict arises, *when* conflict arises—because all relationships suffer conflict. How conflict arises can differ from person to person. We will spend some time educating you on the areas of communication and then discuss alternative methods for communication—including texting, physical touch, and silence. After reading, you may notice your preferred method of communication and how it is similar to or different from your person of interest. Identifying these similarities and differences early on may contribute to your building effective communication as you mature as a couple.

True communication leaves a lot of mystery out of dating. I would be remiss not to acknowledge that men and women may communicate on different levels. Men, you want her to feel invited to ask you questions. Women, allow men the opportunity to ask questions but also make sure they listen to you when you speak.

Some individuals identify with being an introvert, others identify as an extrovert. By adulthood you should certainly know which of these best describes you. That affects how you communicate, too, and I suggest you be certain to let your partner know. If you have a poor method of communication as an individual, this will impact you as a couple as well. There may be a level of dissatisfaction in your union if communication is an issue, leading to still further frustration within the relationship.

Let us agree here that text messages are not a means to build true communication. Emojis do not replace smiling and expressing yourself in real life, face to face. While emojis are cute, they are not designed to replace truthful expression of one's self in person. Apple's FaceTime application is not to be confused with true communication. Although it is fabulous technology, its intent is not to replace in-person face time.

The best way to learn about your person of interest is to effectively communicate. Use the information in this chapter and consider the other ways of communicating as you sit over coffee. This can help can either gain you a lifetime of love or save you a lifetime of misery. Not talking is setting you up for the unknown.

While some say that what you do not know will not hurt you, the other side of the coin is that what you do know can hurt you, too. However, the truth really does have the ability to set you free. Conversation ushers in the possibility of deciding based upon what you do know. The unknown is never meant to help you.

Talking face to face gives you the benefit of seeing the person's body language, facial cues, eyesight, and voice tones. Talking allows you the option of clarifying things that otherwise get miscommunicated or misunderstood. Being misunderstood is especially an issue when using alternate methods of communication. Good old-fashioned face-to-face talking is ideal to build solid communication. Talking is never outdated.

> "Let your conversation be always full of race, seasoned with salt, so that you may know how to answer everyone."
> —*Colossians 4:6 NIV*

When talking, review these four styles of communication:

Passive is to not articulate your needs, messages, and wants. It is undervaluing your need to speak authentically about what you desire. It appears you are under-communicating in order to simply "go along" or "not speak up for yourself." The passive individual will privately take on abusive language to the point of explosion, instead of frequently expressing their needs or responses when others are addressing serious matters. Have you ever heard the expression "Wow, they exploded during our conversation after I made a comment"? That person is likely passive. Over time, things they never spoke up about build up and resulted in that reaction.

Passive-Aggressive is often one of the more treacherous forms of communication, the reason being that during confrontation or conflict the individual may appear agreeable but is harboring a private list of vendettas against you. This individual may not respond in a disgruntled manner while in your presence—in fact, they may appear cynical while convincing you that they are "fine" as a response. However, this is a false "I am fine." Watch and be mindful of the inner anger that speaks to the level of their frustration without ever being spoken truthfully.

Assertive is one who can properly articulate needs, wants, and desires and will appropriately listen to the needs, wants, and desires of their partner. This type of communication happens with confident individuals that may use statements beginning with the word "I." Know that it is okay to communicate your needs and wants. An assertive communicator will portray a unified stance toward others when acceptance of their desires, wants, and needs are embraced by their partner.

Aggressive speaks for itself. An aggressive person communicates in an abusive tone, one very vulgar in nature and directed against you as a person. An aggressive communicator will dismiss your input and opinions and advocate for their needs aggressively. Often verbally, and more than often physically, they will be aggressive when you oppose their demands and advances.

Reflect on the four styles of communication to see which you resemble. If you identify with a particular style and you would like to change, silently pray about your desire for change and work on it. It is possible to change and become an effective communicator in your relationship to be.

Other common ways of communicating are:

Texting is convenient and able to be done on apps, through mobile devices, via chat sessions, and on social media platforms. While texting is convenient, it is not a premier method of communication or a replacement for other methods.

A few things to consider when you are texting:

- o *Initial pursuits (preliminary dating questions) don't benefit from texting.*
- o *Unpleasant news is difficult to convey via text.*
- o *Texting can compound miscommunication.*
- o *Hard topics are difficult to broach over text.*

- *Apologies over text don't carry the same emotional weight.*
- *Breakups over text can leave the situation unclear or ambiguous.*

As you can see, some topics need to be talked about in person rather than sent in a text message.

Consider the following other aspects of communication styles:

Voice tones can determine your mood, whether you are feeling mad, sad, or happy. Be mindful of the pitch of your voice. Think about it: How do you sound when you are happy, sad, or even angry? When you are at peace, happy, or in a good mood your voice tone tends to sound peaceful. And the reverse is also true. Consider whether you want the other person to listen intently. When you are yelling or speaking in a less than respectful tone, it becomes easy to ignore you or end the discussion altogether. You want him or her to listen when you speak. Speaking in a respectful manner does not rob one of their masculinity or femininity. *Talk in a voice tone which will encourage your person of interest to listen!*

Posture communicates your feelings. Does your posture reflect that you are open and affectionate or guarded and closed off? When you are sitting next to your *person of interest*, what does your body posture communicate?

Facial cues can determine mood, feelings, and so forth. If you look guarded or angry, you may appear unapproachable. This is especially true, ladies, when it comes to a man approaching you. Remember your facial cues. What do your facial cues communicate? Are you wearing your angry, "resting B face" or your friendly, pleasant face?

Eye contact when communicating is important. When speaking confidently it is okay to use direct eye contact. Unless culture says otherwise, poor or indirect eye contact can communicate other messages. When answering questions, consider using direct eye contact; when used in conjunction with effective listening, direct eye contact communicates that you are engaged in the conversation.

Body language communicates how you are feeling as well. If you sit in an open posture, it can indicate friendliness. Sitting in a guarded manner—with arms folded or with your fingers pointing—can communicate anger. Even how close you get when speaking with another person can help to indicate whether you're open and friendly or guarded and closed off.

Personal space can be important for those who have issues with respecting others' personal space. Be sure to discuss your individual issues with personal space, especially if you have implemented boundaries for any particular reasons (e.g., trauma). Too many people have been physically or sexually violated, which may directly trigger a person's well-being.

Silence is a form of communication. What can one assume when the other is silent? Silence can communicate a level of non-importance or lack of regard for the other person. Silence is especially an issue after conflict or in regard to unresolved issues. When someone is giving you the silent treatment, it is still a form of communication. The silent treatment can leave issues open to assumption, so keep this in mind as you consider communicating with your partner of interest.

Here are some general questions to help you communicate and guide you to a healthy discussion. Start with these suggestions:

1. Who are you?
2. Where are you going in life?
3. What is your mission in life as a single person?
4. Are you ready for a relationship?
5. What is your ideal vision of your future mate?
6. Are you healed from previous relationship baggage?
7. Which type of baggage do you carry (e.g., obsessive thoughts, anger, resentment)?
8. What is it you expect from me?
9. Do you have any unfinished relationships with anyone else? Any past relationship(s) family, etc. that might hinder *our* relationship?
10. Are you ready to be in a relationship?
11. Where do you see your life five years from now?
12. What does your life look like a year from now?
13. What is important to you at this point of your life?
14. What would you change about my life if possible?
15. What motivates you?

16. Where is your heart's treasure?
17. What are your hobbies?
18. Are you okay dating and marrying outside your race?
19. Do you volunteer, donate money, clothing, etc.?
20. Who do you admire and why?
21. What type of music do you like?
22. What is your favorite TV show and why?
23. What is your favorite movie and why?
24. Do you read? If not, why not? If so, what is your favorite book? What makes it your favorite?
25. Do you admire any artists, musicians, authors, etc.? Why?
26. Define friendship.
27. Do you have a best friend? If so, how long have you known them and what bonds you together in friendship?
28. How do you view male/female platonic relationships?
29. Are you the jealous type?
30. Have you ever been arrested?
31. Have you ever spent time in jail?
32. Do you mind sharing your criminal background report with me?
33. If not, what makes you unable to? (This is for engaged couples or those intending to be engaged).
34. What is happiness?

35. Are you happy?
36. What makes you happy?
37. What makes you sad?
38. Are you quick to anger?
39. Do you like making others happy?
40. Are you judgmental?
41. What is love?
42. What is unconditional love?
43. How important is love to you?
44. Are you an organ donor?

Privately ask yourself the reflective questions below. Some things you need to ponder quietly with the aid of prayer. Spend time meditating on your answers.

45. If you do not see him, take care of himself or herself, do you have any concerns about how they will take care of you?
46. What does your heart say about this person?
47. Do they have any healthy friendships that you are aware of?
48. Have you met any of their friends?
49. What type of friends are they?
50. Do they use alcohol, drugs, etc.?
51. Do you drink alcohol at all?
52. Do you smoke?
53. Do you use any street drugs?
54. Do you have a history of using any drugs?
55. Will you two work out together?
56. How are your diet and eating habits?

57. Do you have any interest in owning your own business?
58. Have you been delivered from any substance abuse?
59. Who are your accountability partners?
60. Do you have an inner circle of close confidants?
61. Do you have a secret service team (aka those who cover and protect you)?
62. Do you think anything is impossible to do in your life?
63. What is important to you at this point in life?
64. Who are the most important people to you at this point in life?
65. What changes do you want to see take place in your life?
66. Are you doing anything daily to execute the changes you want to see?
67. Is there anything in life you are ashamed of?
68. Who can you stand in front of naked, without an emotional mask on?
69. Who are you in private? Ask yourself.
70. What is your personal truth about yourself? Do you only see yourself worthy of less than the best? Do you struggle with a poor perception of yourself?
71. How is this decision—being with them or not being with them—going to affect me in ten years?

72. If I could see inside your heart, what would I see?
73. Who would be the perfect mate for me? Be honest with yourself about this question.
74. What will we do together?
75. What connects us?
76. What unresolved issues do you have in your life?
77. Do we have any resolved issues in our relationship?
78. What makes you cry?
79. Who is there for you?
80. Ask three people: How do you see me?
81. Am I happy because of this relationship?
82. Was I happy before I came into this relationship?
83. Do I make you happy?
84. Are you satisfied with you two as a couple?

If you have decided to share your love interest with a friend or even a close relative, what type of feedback have you gotten? Is it Godly counsel? How did the feedback sit with you? Did it make you feel better or did it make you feel indifferent about your love interest? *Proverbs 13:20* says, "He who walks with the wise grows with the wise, but a companion of fools suffers harm." Seek counsel from those who have modeled relationships you desire to have in your own life. A friend, even if very close, who has a bad relationship or has never experienced a good, healthy,

God-based relationship is not the one to seek counsel from. Also hurting, broken people cannot counsel you. Think about that. I challenge you to find three powerful friendships to counsel you in privacy.

Now that you have asked some questions, consider keeping those responses private and discreet. Sharing with someone about real life requires they know they can trust you with the truth. *Galatians 6:2* says to "bear one another's burdens and so fulfill the law of Christ." When someone significant shares their intimate thoughts, do not tell these secrets to your family, friends, coworkers, or anyone who will listen. At an appointed time, after a committed relationship had been established, they obviously felt the need to confide. What type of example are you setting if they cannot discuss real matters of the heart with you? *Proverbs 20:5* says, "Though good advice lies deep within a person's heart, the wise draw it out."

In other words, be discreet when discussing your relationship woes with people. This is especially important when the person you're talking with is not of mature moral fabric and may not have ever had a relationship of your type, or any serious relationship at all. Airing the flaws of your love interest is, at times, unforgivable if the secrets are extremely personal. It ruins trust. Remember this when discussing your love interest with your family. They do not forgive easily, even though you may.

"Be transparent to the right people and discreet to the wrong people."
—*Anonymous*

Beyond this chapter, consider other resources you and your partner can use to define your method of communication, including individual personality assessments and couple's assessments. Know that communication is a driving force in a well-rounded relationship. A lack of communication is one of the premier reasons that couples do not make it in a relationship!

Communication is key!

Reflections:

Relate-2-Connect Card Deck© "Faith"

"Two is better than one."
—*Ecclesiastes 4:9*

Do you want a partner in the same faith group? If you both are believers in the same faith-based group, this section will be easy to complete with your love interest. Below are a series of questions. I would recommend you pray about committing to sitting down and asking these questions; emotional bonding is easy when you interact with the opposite gender.

1. What is your mission in life?
2. What is your purpose?
3. Are you serving in ministry?
4. Do you attend weekly church and Bible study? Why or why not?
5. Are you saved?
6. How long have you been saved (if a Christian)?
7. Describe your religious beliefs?
8. Are you a Christian? If not, what faith-based denomination do you profess?
9. Are you serving in your faith group if not Christian?
10. If so, which ministry?
11. If not, why not?

12. Do you know your spiritual gifts? (See *1 Corinthians 12*)
13. Are you walking in your purpose or God's will for your life?
14. If a man, are you prepared to be the head and not the tail of the family? (See Ephesians 5:23.)
15. If a woman, do you understand the term "submission" as it relates to becoming a wife? (See Ephesians 5:22.)
16. Have you asked God to show you YOU before you began to desire becoming a mate to another? Spend some time asking God to show you habits that are not appealing to others that may cause discomfort in a marriage (e.g., habitual spending, unhealthy lifestyles, lack of nutrition, diet, exercise, etc.).
17. Do you believe we should be equally yoked? (See Amos 3:3, 2 Corinthians 6:14.)
18. What is your favorite scripture and why?
19. What does the name Jesus Christ mean to you?
20. What does the name God represent for you?
21. Are you a tither? If not, why not? If so, why?
22. Are you supporting your ministry in any way?
23. When you are married, what is your vision for the household as it relates to church?
24. Will you fellowship together or separately?
25. Are you okay dating or marrying outside your faith?
26. Who makes final decisions as a couple?
27. How do you feel about pre-marital sex?

28. Are you celibate or practicing abstinence?
29. What do you know about soul ties?
30. Do you have any family history of ministry roles in the church?
31. Did you grow up going to church?
32. Have you been baptized as a child or an adult?
33. How do you view Holy Communion?
34. How do you feel about missionary trips?
35. What is God saying to you about your life?
36. Do you pray often?
37. How would you describe your faith walk?
38. Are you obedient when God tells you to do something?
39. What is the Holy Spirit telling me about this person? I must be honest to me before I can be to them.
40. Do you know the fruits of the spirit?
41. Do you know the Beatitudes?
42. Do you see God in your mate to be?
43. Do you recognize God in yourself?
44. Do others see God in you?
45. Are you a giver?
46. What is in your heart to do for others (assuming this is not private)?
47. Will you die in your flesh to have a healthy relationship with me?
48. Have you asked God, "Is this the person for me?"
49. What would you like to accomplish in God's kingdom together as a couple?

50. If we need it in the future, are you open to speaking with another marriage mentor couple?
51. Are you open to seeking pre-marital counseling?
52. Do you want your mate to serve with you in ministry if you have a ministerial role?
53. If your partner is not of the same faith, will this be an issue in the relationship?

Reflections:

Relate-2-Connect Card Deck©
"Family"

"Know your roots!"

It is important to know your family heritage. If possible, get a genogram or ancestry report so you will be able to explore three or four generations on both of your parents' sides of the family. It benefits you to know your history and how you have become you. It also benefits you to know about your growing love interest. As one would say, "know your roots." Know their roots, too, if this is to be a potential spouse. When you know your family heritage as it relates to generational blessings, curses, family patterns, spiritual roots, etc., it helps you recognize present day behaviors in yourself and your spouse.

(If you are single parent seeking a relationship, you need to discuss how your union will be affected by becoming a blended family. I explore that further in the *Blender Workshop,* a workshop for daters with kids gathering data to help make it all work in a relationship.)

Have you thought about the family tree that you come from versus the family tree you want to associate with in your future? It may appear that this is too much information but be mindful of, but "I do" means "yes" to the family, too. All the family matters, especially when and if children are involved.

For an up-close experience, go spend time with your love interest's family. Meeting the family offers a wealth of things to see beyond just reading and talking. Observe the family's interactions and the way your love interest communicates with their children (if any), their siblings, their parents, their former wife, their former husband?

Here are some reflective questions:

1. What is the household role of the man?
2. What is the household role of the woman?
3. How is your relationship with your mother?
4. How is your relationship with your father?
5. How is your relationship with your grandparents?
6. What type of family did your grow up in?
7. What was the order of your family?
8. Any family history of divorce?
9. Any family history of domestic violence?
10. Who pays what bills in the marriage?
11. What expectations will you have when you marry if the wife becomes pregnant? Will she work, will she stay home during pregnancy, will she work after the baby is born?
12. Who will discipline the children?

13. Who will discipline children from other relationships (i.e., stepchildren)?
14. How do you feel about dating or marrying someone with children?
15. What holiday traditions will you set as a family once married?
16. Do you have siblings?
17. Are you close to them?
18. What does our life look like together to you?
19. Will this union make you a better person?
20. Any family history of alcohol or substance abuse?
21. Describe your grandfathers on both sides.
22. What type of generational blessings are in your family?
23. What type of unhealthy patterns are in your family that you are aware of?
24. Who will cook and do grocery shopping?
25. Do you know how to cook?
26. How do you feel about leftovers?
27. How do you feel about take-out food every day?
28. Do you know what your parents or grandparents struggled with?
29. Was infidelity a part of your family history? If so, where in the family tree is infidelity?
30. What is your worst fear about your family?

"Know your family roots.

And your love interest's family too!"

Reflections:

"My people are destroyed from a lack of knowledge."
—*Hosea 4:6*

If you are dating outside of your race or culture, it is especially important to ask questions to gain a thorough understanding of how things work for the love interest in your life. I realize this may be an intimidating practice for some, but you must get an understanding so that the relationship can survive the embryonic state. Otherwise, you leave things to chance and the relationship may not survive. If you are timid in nature, use this resource as a guide to gain understanding. At worst, the individual will reject the idea of allowing you to get to know them and that will be revelatory in itself! Trust God in this process and do not leave prayer out of the process.

Do not be afraid. Ask questions!

Reflections:

Relate-2-Connect Card Deck©
"Finances"

"Show me the money."

Surely, this is an interesting subject that impacts relationships and, most importantly, marriages. Ladies, I have to say that you need reinforcement in this area—or at least some of you may. You see, the double standard is that women are not supposed to initiate conversations about money, but I encourage both men and women to discuss money here with confidence. Learn the financial spending habits of your partner, their gendered ideologies behind money, and so forth. Worst case scenario, you learn that money and your boo have no relationship and a lot of money gets misused, abused, or unearned.

Below are some pointed questions to help you learn about your love interest's purse and wallet habits. Sit back, have a glass of your favorite beverage, and discuss the Benjamins, baby! Show me the money! Let's go:

1. What do you do to earn money?
2. Do you work as a contractor?
3. Are you an employee?

4. If you are an employee, do you have benefits?
5. Do you have sustainable retirement income?
6. Define wealth.
7. Define prosperity.
8. How do you view your finances?
9. What is your credit rating?
10. Do you mind sharing a credit report with me?
11. Do you plan to financially contribute to the marital household?
12. Are you okay if your spouse earns more income than you?
13. Do you have any savings?
14. What is your annual income range?
15. Will we combine financial resources?
16. Who will take on most of our financial expenses when married?

"Truth requires trust."

Can they trust you with their truth?

As you have been talking, are you able to keep the intimate details they shared in their responses?

Reflections:

Relate-2-Connect Card Deck©
"Sex"

"Love gives, lust takes."

If you know you are not ready for a sexual relationship, be sure to let your person of interest know that up front. If you are timid about discussing sex, this is not the time to be. Some may think that love is passion during a great sex session (during "*sexercising*"), but that is far from the truth. Have you compared the definitions love and sex in the Bible verses to sex? That's right. The two do not match.

Google defines sex as "sexual contact between individuals involving penetration, especially the insertion of a man's erect penis into a woman's vagina, typically culminating in orgasm and the ejaculation of semen." Merriam-Webster defines love as "strong affection for another arising out of kinship or personal ties" and, further, "attraction based on sexual desire: affection and tenderness felt by lovers."

The best definition of love from the Bible is in *1 Corinthians 13:1*: "Love is patient, love is kind. It does not envy, it does not boast, it is not proud. It is not rude, it is not self-seeking, it is not easily angered, it keeps no record of wrongs." To know the difference is relevant in your connection.

Here are some questions for your sexual discussion:

1. Are you a virgin?
2. Have you been tested for HIV and other STDs?
3. How often do you get screened?
4. After marriage, will we use contraceptives during sex. Why or why not?
5. Who should initiate sex in this relationship?
6. Should anyone in the marriage refuse the initiating party for sex?
7. Define intimacy.
8. Define romance.
9. If our relationship got serious or even led to engagement, would you mind sharing your most recent STD report with me?
10. Are you open to different sexual positions?
11. What are your thoughts on oral sex?
12. What are your thoughts on masturbation?
13. What are your thoughts on masturbation within a relationship?
14. Do you like porn?
15. Do you like watching porn alone?
16. Do you like watching porn as a couple?
17. What do you think of BDSM? (Look it up if you do not know what this term means.)
18. Are you open to others being in the sexual bed with us as a couple? If so, tell me more. If you are not open to it, tell me more.
19. Do you consider yourself a sexual freak? If so, tell me more about that.

20. Are you into sex whenever and however we can as a couple, or does it need to be always conventional at home and only scheduled in the same bed?
21. Will you be offended if I watch porn first or watch porn during sex?
22. Can we have sex in different places? If not, tell me what makes you hesitant.
23. If we could have sex anywhere, where would you want to have it?
24. Can I masturbate in front of you or would that offend you?
25. Ladies, ask him, "Do you want me to wear lingerie?"
26. Do we need to wear protection every time we have sex?
27. Men, ask her, "Are you on birth control"? If she is not, then ask what her position is on birth control.
28. Are you looking to get pregnant?
29. Men, ask her, "Can you have kids?"
30. How often will we make love once married?

1 Corinthians 6:15-20 (NIV)

15 Do you not know that your bodies are members of Christ himself? Shall I then take the members of Christ and unite them with a prostitute? Never! **16** Do you not know that he who unites himself with a prostitute is one with her in body? For it is said, "The two will become one flesh." **17** But whoever is united with the Lord is one with him in spirit. **18** Flee from sexual immorality. All other sins a person commits are outside the body, but whoever sins sexually, sins against their own body. **19** Do you not know that your bodies are temples of the Holy Spirit, who is in you, whom you have received from God? You are not your own; **20** you were bought at a price. Therefore, honor God with your bodies.

Reflections:

Now that you have assessed the situation and engaged in a discussion and asked relevant questions, how do you feel? Do you find that you and your love interest have many things in common? Do you agree in vital areas that provide for longevity in relationships, such as finances, faith, family, friends, and sex?

If you find that this questionnaire has revealed that you two are not quite compatible for a long-term relationship, do not be discouraged. You must believe that the right relationship and partner is available for you. Be and stay encouraged. I leave you for now with this scripture:

> "But those who hope in the Lord will renew their strength. They will soar on wings like Eagles; they will run and not grow weary; they will walk and not be faint."
> —*Isaiah 40:31*

Reflections:

Meet the Author!

Felicia, affectionately known as *Queen Dreamz*, holds a Bachelor of Science degree in Psychology and Christian Counseling as well as a Master's degree in Marriage and Family Therapy from Liberty University.

Smith is the Founder of Relate-2-Clinic, where she works as a Licensed Professional Counselor. As an active Counselor, Advocate, and Inspirational Speaker, Felicia's mission is to work to promote the sound mental health of families.

Author Catalog

Through the Eyes of a Daughter: Fathers We Need You (2012)

Seeds of Hope (2015)

Loving You Feels Right But I Don't Want to be Wrong (2016)

Relate-2-Connect Card Deck© *(2021)*

To follow up with Felicia Smith, MA, LPC, aka Queen Dreamz please visit www.queendreamz.com or www.relate2clinic.org for more information.

> "Mercy, peace, and love be yours in abundance."
>
> —*Jude 1:2*

www.ingramcontent.com/pod-product-compliance
Lightning Source LLC
Chambersburg PA
CBHW030904170426
43193CB00009BA/732